A Tale of Two Cities

Adapted by
Mary Sebag-Montefiore

Illustrated by Barry Ablett

Reading consultant: Alison Kelly
Roehampton University

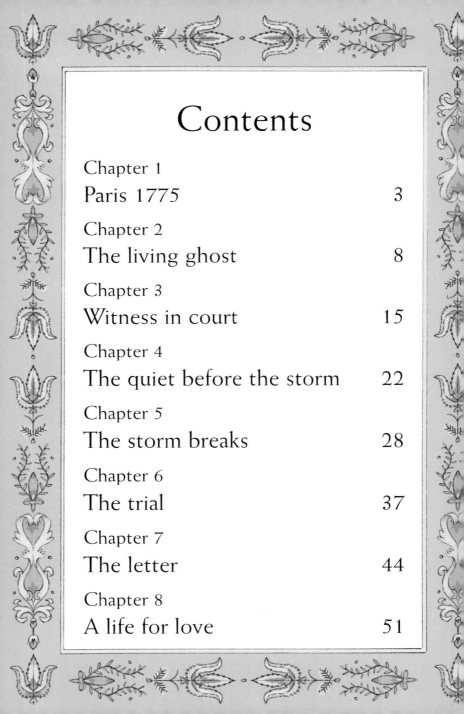

Contents

Chapter 1

Paris 1775

"Out of my way, peasants!" The Marquis d'Evrémonde stuck his head out of his golden carriage as it thundered over the cobbles.

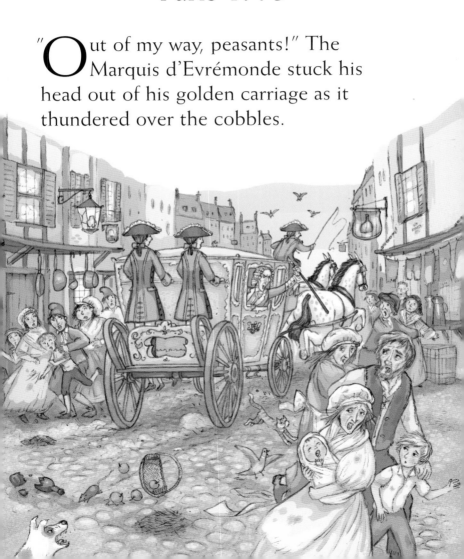

"My baby," shrieked a woman, snatching up her toddler from under the murdering, careless wheels.

"What's one brat more or less?" drawled the marquis, tossing the woman a coin. "Now you have fewer mouths to feed. I hope it hasn't injured my horses."

As he swept past, the woman broke down, weeping bitterly over the still, little body.

"Another Evrémonde crime," Madame Defarge announced, knitting busily. She sat on a chair outside her wine shop, watched by a man unloading wine casks. Click! Click! Click! went her needles.

"What are you knitting?" he asked.

With a sinister smile, Madame Defarge stroked her work lovingly. "Names," she replied, stretching it out. "See – Evrémonde's name is already knitted in. This way, we know who we will punish… one day… when we are ready…"

As the man looked, a wine cask slipped from his arms, smashing into fragments. A red river of wine flowed down the street.

Instantly, all the people within reach rushed to drink it up. They were wild-looking, ragged and gaunt with hunger. With screams of pleasure, some knelt to scoop their hands in it; some sucked the splintered wood; others dipped rags in it and squeezed the drops down their throats.

One man, laughing crazily, plunged his finger in the dirty crimson liquid and scrawled on a wall the word: BLOOD.

The day was to come when that too would be spilled on the streets, and the stain of it would lie red upon the stones...

...because it was the best of times and the worst of times. The rich feasted in palaces while the poor scrabbled like rats for food in the gutter. And while the poor suffered, they dreamed of Revolution, to stop the happy, easy life of the rich, who smiled and danced and dreamed of parties.

Chapter 2

The living ghost

"This is the place," whispered Lucie Manette, her eyes alight with excitement and a little fear. She stepped through the puddles of wine, past Madame Defarge, into the shop.

"Excuse me," she said hesitantly to the man behind the counter. "I've heard that my father, Dr. Manette, is here."

"So he is," said Monsieur Defarge. "Come with me."

"Then it's true," gasped Lucie. "He really is alive?"

"Only just. He's been imprisoned in the Bastille for eighteen years. When he was set free, we brought him here for safety... and to plan our revenge."

"Careful what you say," warned Madame Defarge. "The girl's a stranger..."

"A long time ago, I was your father's servant," Monsieur Defarge continued. "He was a good man, a doctor. Everybody loved your father."

A strange emptiness swept over Lucie as she tried to imagine what eighteen years of captivity would do to a man. "*Was* a good man? Is he... not well?"

Monsieur Defarge was silent, and took Lucie up the stairs. At the top, he unlocked the attic door.

"You lock him in?" Lucie was appalled.

"He knows nothing else. He'd be terrified – rave – tear himself to pieces if the door was left open."

"That's awful," she thought, shuddering with dread. "Awful... I must be brave."

As she entered the attic she saw a white-haired man, with a white beard and a hollow face, sitting on a bench in the window. He was stooped forward, completely engrossed, making shoes.

"Hard at work, I see," said Monsieur Defarge, gently.

After a long pause the head was lifted. "Yes."

The voice was faint, like a feeble echo of a sound made long ago. The eyes looked up, not with any interest, but with a dull, mechanical glance, then returned to gaze at the shoe in his hand.

"Where did you learn to make shoes?" asked Monsieur Defarge.

"Here... in prison... I asked leave to..." said the faraway voice.

"I have a visitor for you. Can you tell her your name?"

A weary sigh. "One Hundred and Five, North Tower."

"He doesn't know his name?" said Lucie.

The man seized his knife, pointing it at Lucie, gasping, "What... who... is this?"

Monsieur Defarge leapt forward to protect her, but she was not afraid.

She folded her father's hands in hers, and kissed them.

Wonderingly, he touched her long golden hair. "My wife had hair like this! Are you an angel?"

Lucie burst into tears. "I am your daughter!" she sobbed, hugging him. "My mother is dead, but you — oh! You shall be restored to life, I promise. Come back with me to England, to be at peace."

He collapsed on the floor. Lucie knelt too, cradling his head, her hair shielding him like a soft curtain. "Please," she implored Monsieur Defarge, "Get us away from Paris now, this instant."

"I'm not sure he's well enough."

"Better to risk the journey than to stay one more hour in this terrible city where he has suffered so much."

"Well, I wish you luck, Lucie Manette." Monsieur Defarge helped the old man to his feet. "Are you glad to be restored to life?" he asked him.

Back came the answer in that faraway, sunken voice. "I don't know."

Chapter 3

Witness in court

The journey back to England was hard, but Lucie and her father were helped by a fellow passenger, a man named Charles Darnay.

Five years later, Dr. Manette was a different man, strong and healthy, and working as a doctor again. He and Lucie lived in a nice little house in London with a quiet, pretty garden.

"Please God," Lucie prayed daily, "Let the bad times be forgotten forever." But then, one day, a summons came through the door.

Dr. Manette and Lucie Manette must attend the Royal Courts of Justice as witnesses in a trial for treason.

They had no choice but to obey. The man on trial was Charles Darnay. Now they learned that he was suspected of being a spy...

"Answer truthfully," a lawyer told Lucie. "Have you seen this man before?"

Lucie stared at the prisoner with pity and admiration. She hesitated, painfully aware the punishment for spying was hanging. "Yes," came her whisper.

"Go on," ordered the lawyer.

"We met him on the boat from France. He was so kind... My father was very ill, and he helped me look after him."

"Did he have papers with him?"

"Yes, I think so..."

"Hmm..." The lawyer paused.

Suddenly, another lawyer stood up. "Look at the prisoner, my Lord, and look at me. Are we not like twins? No one could say for certain that Mr. Darnay was not myself, Sydney Carton, or that Sydney Carton was not Mr. Charles Darnay! No one could be sure, therefore, that it was Mr. Darnay on the boat. Perhaps I ought to be charged with treason too."

Everyone in court laughed. The two men did look extraordinarily like each other, though Sydney Carton was untidy and slouching, while Charles Darnay was upright and much cleaner.

The judge thumped his fist on his desk. "Case dismissed. The prisoner is acquitted."

Afterwards, Sydney Carton came across Charles in the corridor.

"Thank you – with all my heart!" Charles exclaimed. "You helped a complete stranger."

"It was nothing," laughed Sydney. "Tell me – are you a spy? You're French..."

"Half French; my mother was English. Of course I'm not a spy. I'm a French teacher, and loyal to Britain."

"So how does it feel," asked Sydney lowering his voice, "when a golden-haired doll like Miss Lucie Manette can't take her eyes off you?"

Charles flushed. "How dare you..." he began.

"Don't be offended." Sydney slapped him on the back. "And don't be so moral! I'm a bit drunk. I usually am. Life's too dull, otherwise."

He strolled off, looking back as people pressed up to Charles, congratulating him on his narrow escape from death.

Now Lucie was shaking Charles's hand, blushing as she smiled up at him.

"I bet they're arranging to meet again," Sydney muttered, watching them. "He's everything I'm not... more handsome... easy, pleasing manners. If only I were him, a pretty pair of blue eyes would be smiling on me. Huh!"

For comfort he went to a pub, drank a pint of wine, and fell fast asleep. The candles burned down, dripping wax onto his hair as it straggled all over the table, but Sydney Carton, the brilliant lawyer whose laziness had ruined every chance life had offered, didn't know and didn't care.

Chapter 4

The quiet before the storm

The Manettes asked Charles Darnay to visit them. Lucie suggested they ask Sydney too. It was the first of many tea parties, under the weeping willow in the Manettes' peaceful London garden. Sydney began to admire Lucie, not just for her beauty, but for her sweetness and strength of character.

It was obvious, though, that she loved Charles. Sydney grew increasingly moody and hated himself for it, but his feelings for Lucie and his jealousy of Charles made it hard for him to stop.

"I'd do anything for you," he told her one day.

"Please don't say that," she begged, not wanting to hurt him.

"Charles is a fine man, better than I could ever be."

"Couldn't you... try to drink less, work harder...?"

She was surprised to see tears in his eyes. Never had she seen him so softened. It gave her confidence to go on. "I believe in you, Sydney. I wish I could help you..."

"You have... you inspire me. You make me think about starting again... but it's all a dream. I'm like one who has died young – wasted, drunk... I'm glad you don't love me; I'd drag you down with me."

Lucie, desperately sad for him, tried to find words to comfort him. Sydney interrupted her silence. "I know you will marry Charles. Remember this, though. I'd give my life to make you happy. Keep this conversation secret. God bless you."

Soon after, Lucie accepted Charles Darnay's proposal of marriage.

"Now I must ask your father's permission," Charles said. He found Dr. Manette working in the garden.

"I know how much Lucie loves you," he told the Doctor, "and I never want to come between you." He spoke of his desire to marry Lucie and started to explain his background. "You know I'm half French..."

"Stop!" shuddered Dr. Manette. "I don't want to hear about France, ever again."

"I must tell you. Darnay isn't my real name; it's my mother's. My real name is Evrémonde. My uncle is the Marquis, and I am his heir. But I hate his cruelty, and that's why I've made a new life for myself in England."

"Oh God in Heaven... not that name..."
Evrémonde. It jerked Dr. Manette's
memory, recalling everything he wanted
to forget. Time swung back, and he was
once again inside One Hundred and Five,
North Tower, that cell where he had been
buried alive for so many years and all hope
of freedom and happiness had vanished in
the darkness. It was an Evrémonde who
had put him there. Now Lucie would
marry another Evrémonde.

He stumbled into the house, fighting
for breath, struggling with the pain of
remembering. Then, overcome by the
nightmare of prison, his mind went blank.

"Father... where are you?"
Silence.

Lucie had searched everywhere without success. Finally, up in the attic she heard a faint tap, tap. And again, tap, tap, tap. She rushed upstairs and opened the door.

There was her father, silhouetted against the window, bent over his tools. He was making shoes.

Chapter 5

The storm breaks

B ravely, Dr. Manette recovered a
second time from his madness. Lucie
and Charles married, and had a little girl,
also named Lucie, as golden-haired as her
mother.

They were happy days in that London
house, until a letter came for Charles from
France. Reading it, his face grew white
as ashes.

"What is it, dearest?" asked Lucie.

"I must go to Paris at once."

"Please — no!" said Lucie. "We hear of such terrible things in France now. There will be a revolution, everyone says. You won't be safe."

"I must," Charles repeated. "This letter is about an old servant who was good to me. He's been thrown in prison just because he was employed by my uncle. The letter says my uncle is dead. I'm the Marquis now and it's my duty to help this poor man."

"Darling, DON'T go!" Lucie pleaded, throwing her arms around him. "I'm afraid for you."

"Shhh. You know I must do what's right." He was adamant. He kissed his wife and little Lucie, shook Dr. Manette's hand, and went away.

Days, weeks, then months passed, but not a word did they hear from him. Lucie could bear the silence no longer. "If only we were in Paris," she thought, "I'm sure we would find out what's happened to him." She asked Sydney Carton to accompany herself, her fragile old father and her little girl.

"I'll come," said Sydney at once. "Though it'll be dangerous. There are riots everywhere. Paris is becoming a blood bath."

Lucie hugged little Lucie. "No one will hurt us. Everyone knows the story of Dr. Manette, unjustly imprisoned for eighteen years."

She was right... and terribly wrong.

France was in the grip of a revolution. The poor had become a mighty army, seizing power from the rich. The King was tried, found guilty, and beheaded. So were his wife, their children and a thousand rich aristocrats.

The sharp blade of the Guillotine chopped off so many heads that the ground beneath it was soon rotten red, as red as the wine that had once stained the street outside the Defarge's wine shop.

All this time, Madame Defarge had been knitting steadily, knitting the names of everyone to be exterminated. Click! Click! Click! The stitches slipped off her needles as regularly as the Guillotine chopped off heads. Her mouth stretched in a grim line of satisfaction.

"One big fish we still have to catch," she told her husband, "is young Evrémonde, known as Charles Darnay."

"You want him killed too? I hear he has married good Dr. Manette's daughter."

"Every member of that family must die. Now Darnay's uncle, the wicked Marquis, is dead, he'll return to France... and the Guillotine is hungry for him."

"All right, my love," promised Monsieur Defarge. "We just need to find some evidence against him, and I think I know where to look first."

"Where?"

Monsieur Defarge smiled. "Today we storm the Bastille!"

The Bastille! With a roar that sounded as though all the winds of France whistled in that hated word, an army of angry peasants surged to the prison.

Hunger and revenge were their spur; cannon and musket their weapons. Raging fire and smoke blackened the eight great towers and massive stone walls. Wounded soldiers fell into an angry sea of flashing swords, until Defarge and his men swept the drawbridge down.

"Free the prisoners!"

"Unlock the secret cells!"

"Destroy the instruments of torture!"

In the mass of escaping men, Defarge grabbed a prison guard. "Show me One Hundred and Five, North Tower, or I'll cut your throat!"

The terrified guard led him past gloomy cells where daylight had never shone, through hideous doors and dark cages, and up staircases more like dried, crumbling waterfalls than steps.

At last they stopped in a room with four blackened walls, a rusted iron ring in one of them, no window, a worm-eaten stool and a straw bed.

"Pass your torch along these walls," Defarge ordered. In the flickering light he saw initials scratched into the filthy bricks. "A. M." he read. "That's Alexandre Manette. Yes, this was his cell. Hold your torch higher."

A brick in the chimney looked loose. Grabbing a crowbar from the guard's hand, Defarge smashed at it until it gave way. He fumbled in the dusty crevice behind it and drew out an ancient bundle of papers, which he stuffed in his pocket.

"Say your prayers, Darnay," he laughed triumphantly. "These papers may well be your death sentence."

Chapter 6

The trial

Some weeks later, Lucie, her father, little Lucie and Sydney arrived in Paris. Dodging the riots, they went straight to the Defarge wine shop.

"I'm sure they'll help us," Lucie comforted herself. "They were so good to my father."

"Do you know where my husband is?" she asked Madame Defarge.

"I do," said Madame, checking her knitting. "He's in prison, awaiting trial."

"Why?" asked Sydney. "He's done nothing wrong. He only came to France to help an old servant..."

"He's an aristocrat and an Evrémonde. Of course he is guilty. He must die."

"Help me, please," pleaded Lucie. "You are a woman, like me. You know what love means..."

Coldly Madame Defarge stared at her.

"Oh," cried Lucie, drawing her child to her. "I couldn't bear my Lucie to be fatherless. Have pity, I beg you..."

"So this is Evrémonde's child?" Madame Defarge asked, her needles clicking fast. "Her name is in my knitting."

"What does she mean?" asked little Lucie.

"I don't know," whispered Lucie, a chill in her heart.

"As for your suffering," Madame
continued, "why shouldn't you suffer?
Do you think other wives and mothers
have not suffered? All our lives we have
seen poverty, nakedness, sickness, hunger,
thirst, misery. Why should you be special?
Why should we care about you?"

She left the room, leaving Lucie
trembling.

"Don't worry," comforted Sydney. "They can't stop us going to Charles's trial. We'll soon have him free, I'm sure."

"Once the court knows he's my son-in-law, they won't touch him," added Dr. Manette.

They were forbidden to see Charles until his trial. When they arrived in the courtroom, it was already full of onlookers, jostling for seats like a theatre audience. Monsieur and Madame Defarge sat in the front row.

"Charles Evrémonde, called Darnay, step forward," ordered the judge. "I accuse you of being an aristocrat from an evil family who oppressed the poor."

"Cut off his head," roared the crowd.

"But I live in England now," Charles protested. "With my wife, Lucie Manette, only daughter of Dr. Manette, who sits..." he pointed, "...over there."

This answer pleased the crowd. "Dr. Manette," they whispered, "that brave man..." and some had tears in their eyes.

Dr. Manette felt a leap of hope. "If the court remembers me, we have a chance," he thought. Leaning on his walking stick, he stood up.

"Set this man free. He is my son-in-law, a good man, a husband and a father. He does not deserve to die."

"Too late. Charles Darnay is condemned," the judge interrupted.

"By whom?" asked Dr. Manette.

"By Monsieur Defarge, wine seller, by Madame Defarge, his wife, and by one other. Alexandre Manette."

Dr. Manette was stunned into silence.

"Tell the court what you did the day the Bastille was stormed, Monsieur Defarge," directed the judge.

Defarge spoke steadily. "I knew Alexandre Manette was imprisoned in One Hundred and Five, North Tower. I went there. I discovered this letter" – he held up a dusty bundle – "in a hole in the wall. It was written by Dr. Manette."

"Read it to the court," said the judge.

Defarge lifted his voice so that all could hear the terrible words.

Chapter 7

The letter

I, Alexandre Manette, a doctor, have now been in prison for ten years. All hope of freedom is lost. I write with difficulty; my ink is made of scrapings of soot mixed with my blood.

One day a hand may find this letter's hiding place, when I and my sorrows are dust, to learn how I came to this vile and horrible dungeon...

I was strolling in Paris one moonlit night, when a carriage stopped by me. Inside it was a gentleman disguised in a cloak.

"Are you Dr. Manette?" he asked.

"I am."

"Jump into the carriage. I know a patient who needs your care."

I climbed in. We journeyed far, until we reached a deserted house. I heard piteous cries from upstairs, and found a beautiful girl lying tied to a bed, tossing with fever. She was very ill, and after I untied her, I soothed her with medicine from my bag.

Then I heard groans from above. I rushed upstairs into a loft where I saw a handsome peasant boy on some hay on the ground, bleeding. "He's dying!" I said aloud. I turned around to see the gentleman framed in the doorway. "How did this happen?" I demanded.

"A crazy, common dog! He forced me to draw my sword on him."

Not a word of pity in this answer.

The boy's eyes opened and fixed on me. "These nobles are very proud," he rasped, "but us common dogs are proud too. Have you seen her — my sister?"

I nodded.

"We are tenants of this... Marquis," he sneered at the word. "We worked for him without pay while he took our crops, our animals, our hens..."

I was amazed that, though so ill, he summoned the strength to speak. And the Marquis just stood by, completely unmoved.

"When my sister married," the boy continued, "the Marquis saw her, admired her, and asked her husband to lend her to him. When he refused, the Marquis bound him to his carriage, harnessed him like a horse, and whipped him till he fell down dead."

The Marquis shrugged. "These people are animals. They don't have feelings."

The boy's words kept on flowing. "Then he dragged my sister away. I followed them... I bit him, and he struck me with his sword."

With a massive effort the boy sat up and, gasping, raised his right hand. "Marquis," he panted, "I mark you with my blood, as a sign that you and your accursed family must bear responsibility for your wickedness."

With that he fell back, and stopped breathing. I went upstairs to the girl and stayed with her all night, but there was nothing more I could do for her, and when the cold sun's rays shone upon her at daybreak, she too was dead.

The Marquis said not one word to me. We got into the carriage. I expected it to take me home, but instead it brought me here, to this prison, to my living grave. I could not escape.

I believe in the mark of that boy's blood. I believe that the Marquis d'Evrémonde and all his descendants do not deserve God's mercies. I, Alexandre Manette, declare their wickedness to Heaven and to earth.

A terrible sound arose, like the baying of wild dogs in the night. A sound of eagerness that meant blood.

"Save him now, Dr. Manette!" cackled Madame Defarge, in triumph. "Save him now. That dead boy was my brother, that dead girl was my sister. Since Evrémonde killed my family, I have sworn to kill every member of the Evrémonde family. Wind and fire may blow and burn themselves out, but nothing shall stop me!"

At every juryman's vote there was a roar. And another and another. "Guilty!" they cried. Roar after roar. It was unanimous. Charles Darnay was condemned to death.

Chapter 8

A life for love

Lucie screamed. She rushed over to him, and he, leaning over the dock, hugged her.

"Goodbye, my love. One day we shall meet again – in Heaven," he murmured.

"It won't be long. I feel my heart will break. Don't suffer for me, Charles. I will bear everything, while I live."

"Kiss our child for me."

Dr. Manette had followed her and fell on his knees with a cry of anguish.

"No!" cried Charles. "What have you done that you should kneel to us? I understand now the struggle you went through when you learned my real name. Forgive me. There could never be a happy ending for me."

As he was taken away to prison, little Lucie clung to Sydney Carton.

"Oh Sydney," she sobbed. "Can't you think of something to save Daddy? Look at my mother. I can't bear to see her crying like that. Help me... help me..."

She heard him whisper, "A life for love," before he kissed her gently, put her down and followed Charles. That was what she always remembered, years later, when she was an old lady, telling the story to her grandchildren.

Charles, alone in his cell, paced up and down.

He knew there was no hope for him.

The door opened.

"Sydney!" Charles cried, amazed. "How did you get in here? You're not... surely... a prisoner... like me?"

"Certainly not," Sydney said briskly. "I bribed my way in. Now, listen, Charles. You must do exactly what I say. Take off your boots and put on mine."

"This is madness, Sydney. What are you planning? We can't escape from here. You will only die with me."

"I come from your wife and child, Charles. I repeat, do what I say. Now change your coat for mine. Is your hand steady?"

Charles was shaking, but he said, "I think so..."

"Good. Here are pen and ink. Write what I dictate and take it to Lucie. If the wrong people find it, they must think it's a note from you before you died."

Puzzled, Charles obeyed. He dipped his pen in the ink, and wrote Sydney's words.

Remember our conversation long ago. I give my life to make you happy.

"Now put the paper in your pocket, Charles," ordered Sydney.

"What are you doing?" Charles demanded.

Sydney had crushed a capsule in his hand. He thrust it under Charles's nose.

"Whass... that...?" Charles muttered thickly as he breathed in the fumes. He collapsed on the floor, knocked unconscious by Sydney's powerful drug.

"It's worked," Sydney said aloud. He finished changing into Charles's clothes, then opened the door and summoned the guard he had bribed.

"Carry this man out, put him in a carriage, and send him to Dr. Manette, at this address. Now leave me here, in this cell. Lock me in. Hurry..."

The guard did as he was told. The door closed and Sydney was left alone, but not for long. Soon a jailer came in, rubbing his hands with glee, to send the prisoner on his last journey.

Crowds lined the streets, cheering the Guillotine; cheering Liberty, Equality, Fraternity – and Death. As Sydney walked with other prisoners, a girl pushed through to reach his side.

"Can I walk with you, Evrémonde?" she faltered. "I'm so scared. They're executing me for conspiracy, but I've done nothing. I'm only a dressmaker."

"Of course you can walk with me," he smiled, looking down at her. She was very young, and she was shivering.

"Oh," she whispered, shocked, as, returning his gaze, she saw him properly. "You're not Evrémonde!" Then, after a pause, "Are you dying for him?"

"And for his wife and child."

Now she was trembling violently. "May I hold your hand? You're so brave."

Sydney put his arm around her, nestling her head on his shoulder. "You will be brave too," he promised.

"Down, Evrémonde!" yelled the crowd as they walked on. "To the Guillotine, all aristocrats!"

"Is the moment nearly here?" asked the young girl. "Will it hurt?"

"No," Sydney assured her. "It's very quick."

"I feel better with you," she murmured.

Sydney kissed her. "Keep your eyes on me until the end. In the world to come, there is no trouble and no unhappiness. Remember that. Bless you."

Courageously, the young girl met her fate, and then it was Sydney's turn.

They said of him that night that his face was the most peaceful the city had ever seen. He looked like a prophet, shining with wisdom, gladdened by his glimpse of the future. And these were the words he whispered to himself...

I see the lives for which I give my life, safe in my beloved England. I know I shall hold a place in their hearts, and in the hearts of their children. I see my Lucie, an old woman, weeping for me on the anniversary of this day. I see her with a child who will be called by my name. I see this child making a success of his life, not, as I did, ruining every chance I had. I know Lucie will tell this child my story, in her loving, tender voice.

It is a far, far better thing that I do, than I have ever done. It is a far, far better rest that I go to than I have ever known.

Charles Dickens 1812-1870

Charles Dickens lived in London, England, during the reign of Queen Victoria. When he was twelve, he was sent to work in a factory. He never forgot how hard life could be and his novels highlighted the huge gap between the rich and poor.

Dickens went on to become one of the most famous writers of his time. His other tales include *Oliver Twist*, *Great Expectations*, *A Christmas Carol*, *Bleak House* and *David Copperfield*.

Internet links

To find out more about Dickens, life in Victorian times and the French Revolution, go to the Usborne Quicklinks Website at www.usborne-quicklinks.com Read the internet safety guidelines, and then type the keywords "Charles Dickens".

Edited by Katie Daynes
Designed by Michelle Lawrence
Series editor: Lesley Sims
Series designer: Russell Punter